Coloring is a
relaxing, meditative activity
for adults and children.

It's a great way to
relieve stress
and inspire creativity!

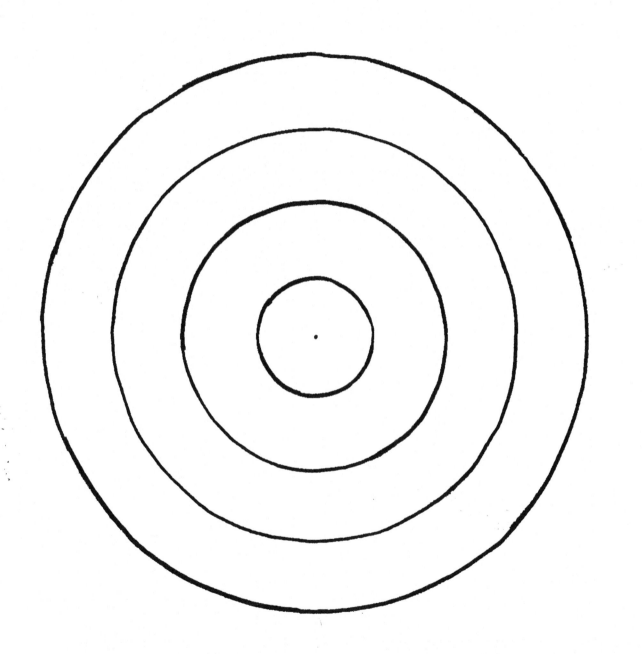

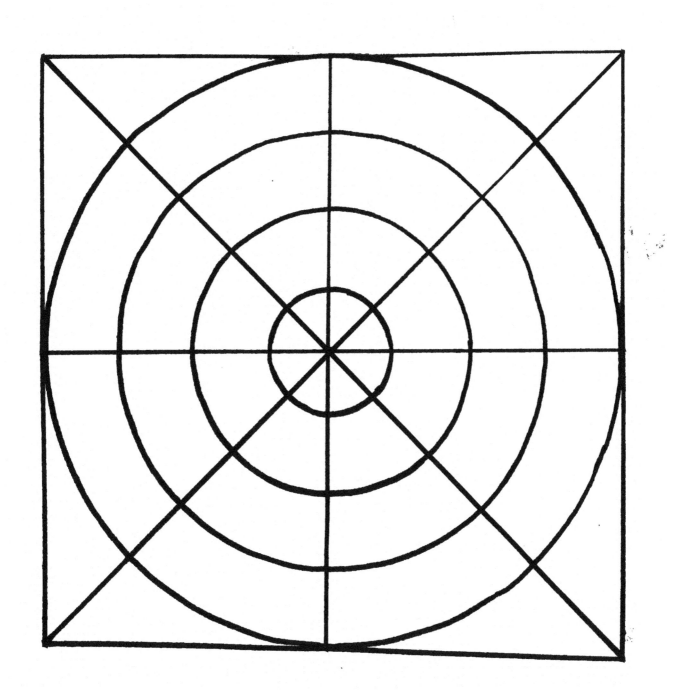

CPSIA information can be obtained
at www.ICGtesting.com
Printed in the USA
BVHW02s2030291117
501448BV00002B/3/P